Traditional Archery Hunting:

stories and advice about traditional bowhunting.

CLAY HAYES

ISBN:149539493X
ISBN-13: 978-1495394935

DEDICATION

This book is dedicated to all those courageous souls that have the stubbornness, fortitude, and heart to follow their own path, whatever it may be.

CONTENTS

ACKNOWLEDGMENTS

There are a lot of people who, either through their guidance, friendship, or both, have influenced this book and myself. For starters, my folks. They aren't the run of the mill variety, thankfully, and allowed me to chase snakes and get dirty as a boy – things that far too few children get to experience today. Jerry Morrell, a good friend and fellow bowyer, has taught me many things about the woods and about life. Lastly, I must thank my wife, and whatever stars aligned to put us together, because I don't think anyone else could tolerate me.

Clay Hayes

INTRO

This collection of stories and practical how to articles comes from a life spent in wild places and among wild things. Within these pages, you'll certainly find some animals that fall to a sharp broadhead, but if you're looking for big scores and big heads (in more ways than one), I'll save you the disappointment. You can stop reading now because you won't find any. What you will find, hopefully, is a love of wildness and hunting that shines through.

I am a hunter. We all are, actually, though many of us either suppress or otherwise ignore the fact. Hunting is what made us who we are and some of us still feel that ancient calling. The stories here are a reflection of that fact, but more so, they're a testament to a love of nature and a desire to be *out there.* Some of the stories, although heavily revised, have been previously published in magazines like *Traditional Bowhunter* and *Primitive Archer.* Others are all new material. I hope you enjoy reading these words nearly as much as I've enjoyed living them.

Thanks and see you in the woods,

ch

Clay Hayes

Frogin' in the Dark

"I see one! Swing the light back around. There! You see him; he's a big'un!" A pair of green eyes glow out of the dark gloom while, all around us, the air is filled with the night sounds of a southern swamp. The collective voice of hundreds of baritone bullfrogs is underscored by hordes of crickets and caped off by a sprinkling of lesser amphibians. I hold the spotlight steady with both hands as Jerry creeps a little closer, testing the limits of his hip waders. "Are you gonna shoot any time soon?" I ask, "Ya get any closer an you could wack him with yer bow. Besides, there's a skeeter nawin on me!"

Bowhunting bullfrogs. It's not something you hear about too often, but when the southern summer days start to heat up, nocturnal pursuits start sounding good. When long time friend Jerry Morrell decided to drive up from Florida for a visit in the midst of a summer heat wave my mind went to working on how to keep us occupied without suffering a heat stroke along the way.

Earlier in the year, while doing some feral hog research over in the Mississippi River Delta, I'd come across this place. I met Mark Cooper, the land manager, who took me on a tour of the private duck club and showed me some places where he'd been having some hog problems (another story). Along the way, I couldn't help but notice the low swampy flooded timber and ditches, so favored by ducks, looked like prime frog habitat as well. I asked Mark about the possibility of a frog hunt, to which he replied – "Yea, dey's lots o'dem slimy SOBs; shoot all ya want!" Cooper is known throughout Yallabusha County for his refinement! If you ever have the pleasure of meeting the man, you'll realize in about 10 seconds what I mean.

The club was a maze of impoundments and ditches with levees running to and fro dividing and connecting the waters and woodlots. Duckweed blanketed the shallow water and, where light could penetrate the canopy of Cypress and Tupelo, water lilies floated. Slides and other sign of beaver were everywhere. Cooper complained, in slightly more colorful terms, that they were a "durn nuisance"; digging holes in his levees and what not.

As we bounced along the levee in Cooper's old pickup, a cottonmouth, who had been basking on a log, slipped quietly into the water – disappearing under the carpet of duckweed. Cooper hadn't noticed, so the 22 resting on the seat between us lay still. The Red-eared sliders, a little farther down the levee, slid off their perch as well, hitting the water with a plop. Daylight in a southern swam can reveal some interesting characters, but it pales in comparison to moonlight. Under the cover of darkness, the swamp relaxes and lets her secrets roam. In a few days, when Jerry and I made it back here, we would have the chance to peek into this hidden world and maybe find some frogs along the way.

When Jerry arrived in Starkville, we packed up and got ready to head west – to the Delta – the next morning. After driving the 2 hours to Greenwood, and putting in a long day of checking out complaints of hog damage, Jerry and I were eager to slip into the hip waders and see what the swamp held. We meet up with Cooper a little after dark. He lets us through the gate and warned "watch out fo da snakes, dey everwhere!", then mumbles something under his breath as he turns back to his truck.

We make it to the first slimy ditch just as the night chorus begins to crank up. A single Green Tree Frog braves the night, letting loose with his two pitched call. This one small frog seems to breach some imperceptible dam and is quickly followed by the hidden hordes, each individual lending his voice to the collective but trying desperately to maintain individuality. The marsh is filled with the incessant calling of tree frogs, leopard frogs, pig frogs, and the unmistakable baritone bass of the American bullfrog, which, by the way, is the largest frog in North America, and the object of our attention on this noisy night.

Bull frogs have been known to reach a pound and a half in bulk. It's not hard to imagine how when you consider that they'll eat just about any moving thing they can stuff into their ample mouths. I've heard reports of them eating mice, small birds, including ducklings, and other amphibians. I once caught one on an 8" soft jerkbait while bass fishing. The frog was floating among some dollar lilies when I flipped the lure over near him. He lunged, mouth open, onto it then used his short front legs to stuff the plastic bait into his mouth. If they were a bit bigger, well, I'd be a little hesitant to be out here. I can see it now, on the cover of the most popular hook & bullet publications: Attack, Killer Frogs of the South! They would, of course, go under the heading of dangerous game.

Despite the future possibility of genetically "enhanced" (the way some want to go with big game) fat frogs striking fear into the hearts of swamp goers, we press on – into the unknown. A little way down the first ditch, the spotlight sweeps across a white throat patch and set of green eyes an inch apart. The frog is facing the water (if you could call it that, it's more like sludge), rear legs drawn up, front legs pigeon toed in that classic bullfrog squat. I ease a little closer, closing the distance to around 5 feet. The old herp shuffles her stance and prepares to launch herself into the slime. Had she been a little quicker on the gas she'd a made it but, as fate would have it, she's now pinned down to the bare mud where she sat, run through by a cedar shaft.

I'd like to say that we were such fine shots that, at those great distances, that we hit our targets with every arrow. The truth, though, isn't so rosy. I guess I started off with a dozen or so mismatched shafts – some short, some long, some heavy or light – all with field tips, which aren't the ideal head for securing a slimy, squirming frog to an arrow shaft.

Some of the frogs had a habit of floating in the matt of duckweed where, if the shot was missed, you'd be hard pressed to find the arrow. The murky, green swamp gobbled up our arrows like they were going out or style. I think I ended up the night with 3 or 4 rather raggedy looking arrows.

We continue on, moving and shining - listening and looking. All in all, it's a nice night, not too many skeeters or snakes and, with the sun to bed, it's not too hot. We're not the only ones working the night shift either. Beaver and muskrat shy from the light, the occasional cottonmouth lies in wait for a wayward frog, and a smallish gator lies in wait for a wayward snake. Out of the murky depths of night comes the hoarse squalls of a couple of lusty coons. It's a wicked sound, half growl, half scream – somewhat reminiscent of a Tasmanian devil, at least the ones I've heard on the Discovery Channel.

A little farther along the levy and a big reddish boar coon waddles out on a log in search for crawdads. Perhaps he's partially the source of the squalls. He's onto us and out of reach before we can get in a position to shoot. The coon's squalling isn't the only peculiar sound to come from the darkness. Beavers slap the water with their paddle like tails and other unseen creatures splash and gurgle in their nightly doings. A night in the swamp is an exercise in listening – imagination fills in what the eyes can't see. The swamp itself is alive and it's a privilege be here, taking part in its pulse.

It's getting late, and we've made it nearly to the last ditch. I've got a few scraggly looking arrows left and Jerry's got about the same. We've had a good night and have 10 big frogs between the two of us. They'll be good breaded and deep fried later on. For the mean time, we've got another hundred yards of swamp ditch to stalk.

Jerry finally feels he's close enough, or maybe it's his waders that decide for him. Either way, he's within a few feet of his target. A quick first shot zips into the ooze an inch left as if into a black hole. "Good luck finding that one", I joke. "Hey, quit gabbin, yer messin up my concentration." Jerry's second arrow finds its mark and the big frog kicks and splashes trying to get away. A sharp crack to the noggin and she's done. The great beast is dead. "Thank god, I thought you were gonna try'n dive on her!" Jerry retorts, "Oh hush up and swing that light over yonder, I just heard one over there. There! You see him, he's a big'un."

Hog Heaven, Literally

Crouching low to the ground, I strain to see through the tangled jungle of briars and pin oak ahead. The cat claw like thorns snag and tear at my bare arms as I make my way towards the commotion barely 40 yards ahead. The briar thicket is so dense that there's no way to stand; no way out but the way I've come; no easy escape from the razor wire tunnel I'm in. Although it's a sunny summer day, no light shines down here. Small beads of blood form in the wake of the briars, but the squeals and soft grunts ahead keep me moving forward, an inch at a time.

The breeze carries the unmistakable sour stench of

wild hogs. I crawl my way the remaining distance to a small opening while concentrating on the movement and sound of hogs jostling for choice resting places. Still on my hands and knees, unable to stand upright, a flicker of movement catches my eye. The swish of a tail attached to a very large grizzled body, laying a mere 15 feet to my left.

Focused on the restless hogs farther ahead, I've inadvertently slipped to within mere feet of a 200 plus pound boar. Other than the occasional swish of his tail, he's still as stone and blends seamlessly with the dark shadows under the briar dome. I want to back away, but there's nowhere to go except back into the razor wire tunnel, and that's not where I want to be when this goes down. I can at least kneel here so I rise to one knee and, steady now, manage to slip a shot through the tangled vines.

The boar explodes with a loud grunt and tears through the wall of briars with brute force sending waves of panic through the rest of the hogs. Chaos ensues as hogs run in all directions. Two sows run back past me into the tunnel I just came out of. The air is clouded with dust and the pungent odor of panicked hog… Then silence. Pondering the situation, I crawl back out the way I had come in and make my way out to the two track road where I can finally stand straight again.

Once back at the truck, I swap my weapon for a tracking box and 3-element antenna. Flipping on the receiver, the familiar beep, beep, beep, gets steadily stronger as the antenna sweeps in the direction the hog fled. This tracking box isn't Cabela's latest in game recovery gadgets. It's a receiver that picks up a signal from the tracking device that the hog is now carrying with him. The truth is, I shot the hog with a small tranquilizer dart fitted with a tiny radio transmitter. Once the boar is unconscious I'll follow the signal to find him, then fit a radio collar around his neck so that I can keep track of him for the next year. And so goes a day in the life of this aspiring wildlife biologist. Tough work, but somebody's got to do it.

While working on my graduate research with Mississippi State University, I spent a year practically living in the field, trapping and tracking wild hogs. I've trapped and darted around 50 wild hogs in the river bottoms near Greenwood Mississippi and followed some of them around, via radio telemetry, to document their habitat use, among other things. All this time spent following pigs through the swamps and briar patches has taught me a thing or two, and I'd like to spin it from a hunter's perspective. Maybe you'll find it of interest, and perhaps learn something along the way. I know I certainly did.

One of the things I've learned over the past year is that hogs are absolutely the perfect quarry for the ground pounding bowhunter. Hogs have poor eye sight, fairly good hearing, and a nose that is unmatched by any other wild game in North America. They are numerous in many parts of the country, especially here in the south. They're most often classified as a nuisance or predatory animals, which often results in very few restrictions on season or bag limits. If that's not enough, wild hogs provide some of the best table fare of any North American game animal, hands down.

Hogs are often found in droves or family groups that are usually composed of 2 or 3 large sows and their offspring. The large boars are frequently loaners, occasionally attaching to one of these droves for a while and then seeking out some other conquest. Hogs are habitually noisy when actively feeding in droves so you shouldn't be overly concerned about making a little noise during a stalk. Numerous times I've walked to within a few feet of hogs feeding in heavy cover without being discovered. The nose is the defense to concern yourself with. I've had many promising stalks come to a frustrating end due to a fickle wind or being in the wrong place. When a hog catches wind of you, they don't hang around to see what's in store.

When there are a good number of hogs in an area, a

little scouting will usually betray their presence. No matter where hogs are in the world, there is one similarity in habitat preference that consistently rises to the top. THICK! No matter what time of the year, hogs like the thickest, nastiest, most uninviting places imaginable. There have been studies in California that show the thicker the vegetation, the more hogs like it.

My hogs often bedded in briar patches where tunnels and trails through the vegetation were clearly evident. During the hot dry summer months they spent most of the day resting in these places, becoming active only at night. When the weather is hot, it's been my experiences that unless you know exactly where a hog is laying, don't bother trying to find them, as they will often lay in their bed motionless, aware or perhaps unaware of your presence.

Your best bet for hot weather is early morning, when it's not so hot and pigs are returning from feeding the night before. Pigs don't sweat, so they have to rely on other means to keep themselves cool. One of these means is to lay around in the shade during the hottest part of the day. Position yourself between active feeding areas and promising bedding spots, and try to intercept the pigs on their way into the thick cover. Once the pigs make it into the thick vegetation, they are not likely to emerge again until dusk or dark.

Food is also a major factor in where hogs will be at different times of the year. In the area where I worked there were a lot of acres in corn and soybeans, as well as countless small food plots planted with everything from millet and oats to clover and ryegrass. Once a group of hogs finds a good source of food they will usually come night after night until the resource is gone, unless disturbed.

During my field season I watched a group of hogs literally destroy a patch of millet intended to be flooded for waterfowl. Every evening at the same time, they would make their way over the levee into the dry pond and feed on the millet all night. With the coming of dawn, they would retreat back into the thick cover to pass away the hottest part of the day. This particular pond was situated adjacent to an old field with lots of nasty cover. There were several heavily used trails coming from the thick brush into the pond and there was hog sign everywhere.

Although there were other millet patches around, this one provided a good source of food within easy reach of their bedding area. I've often seen hogs feed in a food plot or some other food source until satiated, then stagger their way to the nearest thick cover and lay around all day. When evening approaches, they come back to repeat the assault. This tends to bring about a rise in blood pressure for the land managers, but can be a huge asset to hunters.

Once I find a good active feeding area, I'll begin looking for the closest good cover. In areas where there are many hogs, there are often clearly defined trails leading from feeding areas to thick cover. As long as the wind is right, I would normally set up along these trails in the evening to wait for them to emerge from the thick stuff. If you are fortunate enough to find them in an area open enough for a stalk, hold onto your socks. Stalking wild hogs is one of the most exciting and achievable things a bowhunter can undertake.

If legal in your area, baiting can be a particularly effective tactic. After trying nearly everything imaginable to bring hogs to my traps, I can say that soured corn or wheat is undoubtedly the most effective. Fill a couple of 5 gallon buckets with corn, leaving about 5 inches of space at the top for the grain to expand and then fill with water. Cover with a top and set it in the sun for a couple of weeks and you will have the precursor to sourmash whisky. If you take this revoltingly smelly stuff and dump it out in an area with hogs nearby, you can bet it won't last long. Before hunting it, give a couple of days for the hogs to get accustomed to coming to the bait, checking periodically to make sure it's not all gone.

You hear a lot about hunters touting the dangerous nature of hunting wild boars. I've heard tales of fearless tuskers treeing hunters and charging upon first sight. Well, I'm here to tell you that most of that is just a bunch of crap. I've spent immeasurable hours within spitting distance of wild, unimpeded boar hogs, and have never felt unsafe. I think a lot of these tales spawn from trapped or otherwise cornered hogs. If given the opportunity hogs will flee, but when they feel trapped they become very aggressive.

The only time I have ever seen a hog act aggressive toward a human is when they are in a trap. When a hog feels trapped, cornered, or otherwise detained they can be one of the foulest natured beasts on earth. Trapped hogs commonly charge and hit the fence, creating quite a ruckus that would probably scare the heck out of the uninitiated. Although this may sound like I'm downplaying the danger factor associated with bowhunting hogs, I would not underestimate the unpredictability of a wounded or surprised hog; or any large wild animal for that matter.

As table fare, wild hogs are, in my opinion,

unmatched by any north American big game. If I
had my choice, I would like a nice young hog for
the table. Although I've killed some large boars that
were palatable, I've also killed some who's meat
was so rank that one whiff of backstrap in a hot
skillet would turn a skunk green with envy.

One way I've found to test the edibility of a boar is
to cut a small piece of meat off of the carcass and
throw it in a hot skillet. If the meat is too strong, the
stench will be quite evident. It might be best if you
do this outside, as it tends to stink up the house. I've
never found a sow to have this sour stench of a
large boar, though I'm not saying it couldn't
happen. If the weather is warm, take great pains to
get the animal gutted and the hide removed as
quickly as possible, as I think this may contribute to
some of the offensive odor in the meat of large
boars. Don't let all this talk of stinking boars keep
you from sampling wild pork, it may just be the best
you've ever had. Just remember sows and young
boars are your safest bet.

So back to bowhunting. I've hunted hogs in Florida,
Alabama, Mississippi, and Texas, and I never lose
interest. There's always something new. With sight
and hearing less keen than a whitetail's, hogs are
just plain fun to sneak up on.

I've even heard of one guy sporting a black coat and

crawling on all fours to within bowshot of a group of hogs feeding in a wide open corn field. Apparently the pigs thought he was just another porker coming to join the feast. Try that with a whitetail! If you haven't tried stalking wild hogs, you're really missing out. They are truly the perfect quarry for the bow shooter.

Old Oak

For nearly three centuries the old warrior spread his branches toward the sun. His broad crown has shaded this patch of river bottom, turning sunlight to wood and acorns. After three hundred years of dropping mast and holding squirrel nests, his massive old trunk now lay propped solidly against another slightly younger oak. It was caught mid fall at an angle just low enough to allow a hunter to walk up the bole into the crown. Sitting here in the crook of a branch, it's easy to muse about the squirrels and the birds and bucks; about the role this old oak has played and about how that role changed this past September.

After 300 years of hurricanes, he finally succumbed. Being the biggest tree in the woods has its competitive advantages, but it doesn't come without risk. I'm not quite sure what it is about these rare treasures but, when I find one, I can't help but walk up into the branches and sit for a while.

Yesterday morning I bundled my wool blanket, canvas tarp, hatchet, bow-drill, a few beans and some salt pork and tied all to my wooden pack frame. I grabbed my Osage bow and quiver and struck out. With no particular destination in mind I just wanted to get away; out into the woods where I wouldn't see anyone for a few days. The refuge land across the gravel road from my house holds one of the few places around where you could get more than a half mile from a road. If you can get a half mile from a road, you can get a quarter mile from 95% of the hunters.

The deeper into the woods I got, the narrower the trail became. Boot tracks were replaced by those of deer and turkey. I knew this trail and these woods, having spent countless hours exploring and hunting the creeks and pine woods hereabout. I knew the creek made a bend just up ahead and there was a little flat on a small bluff just perfect for a secluded camp. As I crossed the muddy creek on an old familiar log I noticed coon tracks pacing the water's edge. The banks were covered where the old boar had searched for crawfish the night before. Piles of coon scat containing nothing but persimmon seeds and crawfish shells lay here and there. From the size of the sign he's a big one, probably turned red with age as old boars are prone to do. He's probably not far, sleeping the day away in the hollowed trunk of a basswood.

When I reached my bluff, the pack came off. For being homemade it's not bad, but top'o'the line it isn't. I sat for a while, let my shoulders rest, and surveyed the site. It was a lovely little area, high enough to be safe from flood and open enough to afford a nice view of the river bottom below. The leaves had long sense dropped off the hardwoods and the grey trunks of hickory and oak saplings offered the only cover for several hundred yards.

After a little rest I unbound my pack and got started on making camp. There was an old, half rotten pine laying there, offering itself and begging to be made into a windbreak. When the old snag fell, the impact on uneven ground had broken it into several manageable sections. All I had to do was make a cradle of upright posts and stack the broken sections in them, one on top of the other. In just a little while

I had a fine debris wall to block the cold December breeze that I knew would come later at night. With the debris wall finished all I had to do was string up my canvas tarp in a diamond shelter and stuff the mattress bag with pine straw and leaves.

After collecting enough firewood for the night, I grabbed my bow and tried to lose myself and a few arrows as well. There were plenty of squirrels around, but after two months of dodging rimfire most were in the tops of hundred foot pines. Conventional tactics weren't going to work so I went about looking for a natural hide to sit and wait for the little rascals to come down to forage on the fallen oak mast. That's when I found this fallen giant.

I climbed into the branches and sat, a perfect 15 feet above the crunchy leaf litter below. A well used deer trail ran by at 40 yards, well out of my range, but there's plenty of oak mast close by. Having brought only a few beans and saltpork, the idea of fried squirrel and gravy sure sounded nice as I watch the bushy tails in the bare canopy above. But ideas would be all I'd have. After an hour's wait, a single grey squirrel braved the forest floor within bowshot. As I moved to draw, he scrambled a few feet up a nearby hickory and stuck himself there, upside down, pumping his bushy tail and barking.

The field tip hit the hard wood with a crack that sent my dinner back into the clouds from which he came. From the pine thicket to the north came a series of short nasal snorts from an unseen deer. It's quite the thing, the satisfaction a hunter can glean from so close a miss. I tipped my hat and bid my quarry farewell before climbing down and heading back to camp. On my way I noted landmarks to help me find my way back to the old oak in the predawn morning.

Later that night, after a dinner of rice and beans, I lay in my shelter, warmed by a fire by friction, good oak and a coyote's song. I manage to read a page from Walden by flickering firelight before the barred owls began to cut up. There's an old saying in the south about being drunker than a barred owl. It's easy to understand when you've listened to a pair hooting out their strange duet in the river bottom darkness. Most people never get to experience these things. They spend their lives insulated by thick walls and padded comfort. Some may see nature from afar; her surface beauty but rarely any deeper. I'm lucky to have been there, to have *wanted* to be there. I'd give up a warm, soft bed for a chorus like that any night.

The next morning, this morning, I find myself back in my perch. The seat in the old oak isn't perfect by any stretch. I could have hung a stand a little closer to the deer trail, but I'd rather sit here, perched in a piece of history. Logic says to move closer, but logic carries little weight here and now. The first old doe melts out of the pine thicket just after first light. The sudden appearance of game, the cold rush of adrenalin, is one of the great things about hunting. She slips quietly down the worn trail with a big fawn close behind. The pair doesn't step from the trail and pass by out of range.

I sit, content with my natural stand, and watch a brown creeper on his perpetual upward march, searching for insects in the scaly bark of a white oak. An hour passes before I hear footfalls again. I turn slowly to see a slender young doe feeding under a chestnut oak. She looks a little awkward picking up the nearly golf ball sized acorns. She loudly pops one in her jaws and half falls from her mouth. When she's finished with the first half she nimbly reaches down and mouths the second.

With a heavy mast crop, life is good for a deer this year. She's sure safe from me. There's no way I can turn to squeeze a shot through the brown crispy leaves clinging to the branches of my perch. Sometimes I wonder why I ignore obvious disadvantages to climb and sit in a tree like this one. I've never really figured that out, but then again, I don't think I really need to. There are a lot of nuances to why someone would shoot a wood bow, or sit in a fallen oak. Maybe the two are connected; both symptoms of the same affliction.

On hunting from Trees

Hunting from a tree stand is one of the most popular tactics today for one simple reason, it's effective. Nationwide, whitetails are the most popular and widely distributed big game and, in order to beat them consistently, many bowhunters head for the trees every year. I'd argue that becoming a good tree stand hunter requires just as much skill as still hunting or spot and stalk, albeit a different set. A good tree stand hunter sometimes seems to have a sixth sense about animal movement and picking the best stand locations for the time of year and property.

If you're thinking about hunting from a tree stand, the first thing you need to figure out is what type of stand you'll be using. This discussion will be geared toward hang on stands for a few reasons. They are, in my opinion, the simplest, quietest, most versatile type of tree stand out there (aside from a nice, well formed live oak branch). Several hang on stands placed around a hunting area frees a hunter from lugging a climber around (something I suffered through for several years). I like to still hunt to my stands in the afternoon and out in the morning. I just can't do that effectively with a climber on my back. Additionally, they are much quicker and quieter getting into and out of than a climber. Ladder stands are nice but they tend to be expensive and they're difficult to pack for any distance to set up.

When you're picking out a stand, or stands, you should also be thinking about a safety system. I'm a believer that we should be tied into a safety system from the time we leave the ground until we set foot back on terra firma. A quick internet search suggests that somewhere between 50% and 75% of tree stand accidents occur while the hunter is entering or exiting a stand. It's no coincidence that this is precisely when most of us neglect our safety system. I started using a permanent system several years ago (after some bruising and sore ribs) with all of my hang on type stands. It's a simple system, but effective. A length of climbing rope is attached a few feet above the stand and again near the base of the tree. Then a prussic knot (Google it) is tied around this main line. I just clip my safety harness into the prussic and slide it up the main line as I enter the stand. If at any time I happen to misstep and fall, the prussic clinches on the mainline and stops my fall. If you go this route, keep in mind that you need good climbing rope, not just that poly stuff you get from wally world. The force of a fall will exceed your body weight several times and not just any rope will hold up to that kind of pressure.

One of the things that I love about tree stand hunting is that it gives a hunter a vantage point, gets us above the action, and allows us to watch all the forest critters go about their lives as if we weren't even there. That is, if we do it right. One of the downfalls of would be tree standers is the trimming of shooting lanes, or lack thereof. When it comes to trimming up a stand, some folks seem to whack down every sapling within 20 yards, while others scarcely alter a twig.

For me, the trick is to find just the right balance between open areas to shoot, and retaining plenty of cover and a natural look. If you've got a buddy to help trim, take'em along. You'll spend less time trimming, cut less vegetation and have better, more accurately placed shooting lanes in the end. I've found it best to have one guy sitting in the stand, directing the cutter on the ground to offending vegetation. That way, the shooting lanes are trimmed from the hunter's perspective.

It really helps to have a good idea of where the deer are likely to be coming from, so a good knowledge of how they use the area is important. I like to use some of the cut limbs to brush up the area just behind my stand. This helps to break up my outline and conceal movement. Evergreens work best for this since they will retain their foliage for months after being cut. You can also use some of the cuttings to create "micro-funnels" to gently guide critters to one trail or another.

Another thing I like to do while trimming up is to shoot a few arrows from the stand to spots where a deer is likely (hopefully) to be some fateful day in the coming season. This does two things: It's great practice, but more importantly, it's the best way I've found to fine tune those shooting lanes and the area right around the stand. There's nothing like actually shooting from the stand to point out those little twigs that like to jump out in front of an arrow or bow limb at crunch time.

Even in its seemingly narrow scope, the fundamentals of tree stand hunting defy coverage in anything less than an entire book. I've only given a few of the more important (in my mind) basics aspects unique to hunting from a tree stand. There are many, many more issues that I'd consider basic but hardly unique to the method. Things like setting up for wind direction, understanding animal behavior and movement patterns, scent management and more are basic woodsmanship relevant to many hunting methods. The only real way to learn is to get out there and climb a tree. So get goin', and be safe.

Brush Country

South Texas brush country is a fascinating place. To look at it you'd think that it would scarcely support a goat. Everywhere underfoot is bare and cracked clay, hard baked in the brutal sun. What vegetation does manage to suck a living form the parched ground is covered in thorns, it's dryer than hell and just as hot during the summer, but, for some reason, this is one of the most productive places I've ever visited. This region along the southern border, known as the "golden triangle", grows some of the highest scoring white tails in the world, supports flocks of wild turkey, scaled and bobwhite quail, jackrabbits, cottontails, javelina and wild hogs by the droves. But that's just the start. Flip over a stone anywhere and you're likely to uncover any manor of critter from tarantulas and scorpions to some of the largest snakes in North America. The eastern diamondbacks here are enormous and plenty, but they pale in size to the indigo snakes. These iridescent black monsters can reach lengths of eight feet. But it's not only the diversity that is amazing. The sheer numbers of animals is astounding. For a stickbow hunter in the 21st century, there are opportunities everywhere and, if the number of artifacts laying around is any indication, it's been this way for quite some time.

Early morning on the south Texas plain is a special time. It's often the only time to get a glimpse of some of the critters hereabouts. While sitting on the porch watching the sun rise, sipping a steaming cup of coffee, I can't help to think of one of the lines in "A Sand County Almanac" where Leopold wrote, "Getting up too early is a vice habitual in horned owls, stars, geese, and freight trains. Some hunters acquire it from geese, and some coffee pots from hunters. It is strange that of all the multitude of creatures who must rise in the morning at some time, only these few should have discovered the most pleasant and least useful time for doing it." Indeed. I can just see Aldo finishing off a pot, noting the first birds to call and drinking from a blue speck tin cup, just as I'm doing now.

How different though this country is from that fabled sand farm in Wisconsin. I think he would have liked it here, though caracaras and prickly pear are a far cry from the cardinals and oaks he so loved to see. Musing aside, it's a fine morning. It's not too cold, but there's crispness just right for a morning stroll. The small game hunting around here doesn't get much better, and with the always present possibility of running into javelina or hogs, it's enough to get any hunter out of bed and into the brush.

Taking advantage of whatever opportunities arise seems to be a shared trait among traditional shooters. I suppose, with our self imposed handicap, it makes sense to just hunt, anything and everything about. With such a variety of game species around it doesn't make much sense to limit yourself to any one. You sure don't see many compound shooters flinging arrows at squirrels and grouse and their missing out because of it. When the coffee's gone, I head in the house and string up my old longbow, the one I took my first whitetail with just a few years ago.

She's been dragged a lot of miles since then; through swamps and up trees, under water and over the hill. Some would say she's ugly, but, what do they know. A few knots and sinew patches, dried mud and one missing horn nock don't necessarily detract from the beauty of the thing. I grab a few arrows, mostly field tips, some broadheads just in case, and stuff them into a cat skin quiver. With the arrows slung low across my back and bow in hand I set off up the rutted clay road to see what's afoot.

Around here, on a cool morning, you don't have to walk too far to get into some good rabbit hunting and today's no exception. Just a ten minute walk from the house there's a stock pond where the hogs water on occasion. Just beyond that, there's a large prickly pear flat with good cover of blackbrush and some other yet to be identified thorny things. Quiet now, and slow. The first cottontail, hunkered at the edge of a thick stand of pears, ears laid flat in that classic cottontail pose, is coiled and ready for flight yet still as stone. The first shot of the day misses high, sending gravel and dust flying into the thorny green pads beyond the bunny.

Ordinarily, missed shots have a way of making game relocate but cottontails, displaying unwavering faith in unobtrusiveness, often let you get a second shot in. At the shot the bunny takes off for ten feet then stops just as suddenly as he began. Sitting again in that motionless form, just 15 yards and a little more in the open, he's not so lucky on the second go. A center hit strings him half way up the shaft and he's dead before I cover the short distance and pick him up.

Even though this place seems hostile and barren, he's a plump little thing, fat and healthy. I gut him, prop open the cavity with a stick, and tie him to my belt. It's still early but with enough meat for lunch, I drift off my game a little and spook the next two bunnies into the thick brush without even drawing a shaft. When I spook the third, he runs to a far thicket and hesitates just long enough for a 40 yard shot that flies left, then disappears into the thorns. As I bend down to pick up my arrow, a white fleck catches my eye. It looks like a shiny piece of plastic or glass, mostly buried in the clay and oddly out of place in this desolate country.

Forgetting the arrow for a moment, I reach down and wiggle the shard loose from the earth. What I find is no plastic but a perfect, intact arrowhead. After a little spit and shine, the red clay wipes off to reveal the white and pink stone and perfectly serrated edges. The quality of craftsmanship shines through the idle centuries. I sit on the ground and turn the stone over and over in my palm. Finding a relic of ancient times is always fascinating, but when the artifact is a piece of hunting history, it always carries special meaning for me. It always makes me wonder about the man, the one who knapped this tool; who depended on it for his own life. What things he must have seen. How did he come to lose the head? Had he missed his target? Had he been successful? There's a good chance he was hunting with a simple osage selfbow just like the one I'm carrying.

After daydreaming a while my stomach begins to rumble. Roast rabbit over mesquite coals back at the house sounds good, but I've got a better idea. I always carry a spare bowstring in my quiver so with the almost overpowering feeling of nostalgia brought on by finding the arrowhead and daydreaming about the one who made it, I figure I'll make a bow drill, start a friction fire and save myself the trip back to the house. The string comes out, I find a nice curved branch from a nearby mesquite for the bow, find a suitable spinal and fireboard. Up on this hill, all I can find is mesquite. Pretty hard, but it *might* work. The cottonwoods down on the dry creek would be better.

After cutting out a notch (no easy task with mesquite) I set to work with the bow drill. The smoke comes quick and heavy, a little black powder begins forming in the notch. But after several attempts I just can't get a coal and eventually wear the string in two. I can almost feel the flint knapper's presence, standing over my shoulder, shaking his head at my feeble attempts at something that was fundamental to his own survival. Maybe the mesquite is too oily, maybe my technique needs a little work. I'm not sure what exactly the problem is, but I'm sure the flint knapper knows.

Coming Home

They've always been there, in my heart, my soul – calling, beaconing, tugging at my feral core that, for so long, has been shut in by the suffocating confines and stifling humidity of Florida. I was homesick for a place I'd never been, a place where a body could get away from the incessant hum of humanity, the honking horns, barking dogs. It's almost as if I've returned home, perhaps from another life. This country fills an almost imperceptible void deep down in my soul. It was inevitable that I'd find myself here, not a visitor here to bag a bull and retreat to the comforts and subconscious confines of city life, but as a resident – free from the stresses of success and outfitter fees, limited time and the things that weigh on the minds of traveling hunters. These are the things that can make them blind to grouse and aspen leaves, pinecones and juncos. Their visions of antlers and time constraints often seem to block out the little things that make hunting so enjoyable.

I first saw the Rockies in the summer of 95, embroidered on the horizon and shimmering like a mirage across 300 miles of central Wyoming's arid and sun baked flatlands. I swore someday I'd make it there and 12 years later, on the slim prospect of permanent work, I did. The western slope is where I found myself, just 80 miles from the southern reaches of the Yellowstone and in some of the best hunting country in the lower forty eight. For a kid from the south who'd dreamed of elk and grizzlies, pack strings and wall tents, heaven was at hand.

Elk season officially started at 5:23 a.m. three weeks ago and I've hiked up this snowbrush choked hillside at least ten mornings since then. It's amazing how big animals with big antlers can navigate this maze of horizontally growing nastiness while it's all I can do to keep from snagging brush in my bow tips and keep the arrows in my quiver. But navigate they do. Just this morning I glassed a bull on this hillside from my seat on the opposite ridge. The brushy hillside didn't look bad from a quarter mile away so I trudged over here, only to get mired in this maze. Now I'm picking my way along a beaten game trail trying to be as quiet as possible while keeping alert and working the wind.

There's elk sign everywhere – beds, turds, tracks. I can smell them and catch a whiff of that intoxicating barnyard stench that only a hunter can love. You'll usually find an arrow in my bow hand but, in this stuff, where stumbling is pretty common, and I don't want to extract a broadhead from my thigh, the broadheads stay in the hip quiver. Fifteen minutes later, and nearly at the last place I saw the bull the brush pops ahead and a big animal lunges forward just a few yards away. I let slip a cow call and take a few quiet steps into a tiny opening in the brush. A second later, just as I reach the opening, a young cow steps out from the uphill side. I must have jumped her a moment ago and now she's wondering where the calls came from. She steps from the brush and walks just 5 steps from my unprepared self. Knowing the odds of being busted are high, my hand slowly eases toward the hip quiver while the cow walks downhill. By some miracle I manage to get an arrow out and nocked while she's still less than 15 yards away. I could probably make the shot, but she's quartered hard and moving. I give her a mew and she stops and turns at 20 yards. But only her head and neck are showing. She looks back over her shoulder for a moment then steps into the brush and out of sight.

Encounters like this one are one of the big reasons that I so dearly love this game. Sure, I would have loved for her to step broadside when she turned to look for the hidden cow. Or to have had an arrow nocked when she first stepped from the brush broadside at 5 yards. But, I'm not too disappointed. I got the chance, the opportunity to be so close to a wild elk, and had almost beaten her at that ancient game. But such defeats are easily brushed off when the game is played for playing sake.

Just last Saturday I had another very close call with a magnificent herd bull. I glassed him and some cows topping a ridge and heading into a timbered drainage the night before. About daybreak the next morning with the wind moving down the draw, I got down below them and still hunted my way up toward the ridge.

There was fresh sign everywhere and their scent drifted down on the breeze. I eased my way up, following fresh tracks, elk stink, and wet mud on vegetation. I followed them until about 11 am. Shortly after I sat down for a rest and a snack a bugle rolled in from just over a small knoll. I shouldered my pack, eased over the break and could hear the cows mewing, snapping branches and knocking hooves on the deadfall. I eased in a little closer – across the crunchy, fir cone littered ground – and crossed my fingers that one would feed to me before I got busted. By this time, the bull was really firing off. It's stunning to be so close to such a magnificent animal and to get to hear all the deep guttural noises they make. I could almost feel him.

I kneeled there as a spectator, watching the cows feed; watching the bull tend his harem, rounding up a stray cow then running to the other end of the herd, grunting and posturing the whole way. After a few minutes a cow walked directly at me, spotting me when she got to within about 5 yards. I would have taken the shot had she presented me one but she stared then backed straight away, wheeled around and flashed back into the midst of the herd. Apparently she wasn't too alarmed because she didn't blow the whistle. Some of the other cows and calves had, by then, meandered down below me and were threatening to pick up my scent stream. I crossed my fingers and hoped. Just then the bull started up the hill, just to my right. Could it happen, could I be this lucky? The bull heads to where the first cow had come from and then turns toward me, stopping a mere 8 yards away. His massive head and shoulders are covered by a big gnarly fir as he looks down on his harem, unconscious of the danger so near.

Eight yards and 2 steps forward is all that separates me from putting an arrow into this monarch. But it wasn't to be. My stars weren't aligned or maybe that cow walked just a little too far and caught my scent, but in a moment all hell broke loose. The cows from below took off, crashing away up the draw. The bull threw up his head, watched for a half second then wheeled and was gone, leaving me in a surreal haze. I opened my pack and had lunch.

What a rush it is to be a predator on the brink of a kill – hidden in ambush, every ounce of focus intent on the game with senses burning for it. That feeling, and I don't know exactly what to call it, is as natural to modern humans as it to a lion – waiting, crouched with muscles quivering in anticipation of the final lunge. That's tunnel vision on high but I fear, today, most hunters never experience it. It's a feeling that comes only after penetrating the games defenses, millions of years in the making; defenses that have been honed, sharpened, and tested by predators much more skillful than himself. Nothing else matters at that moment but predator and prey. Fortunes hang by the finest threads and thankfully so. How drab a vocation hunting would be if those threads were a bit stouter, binding fortune to less uncertain outcomes.

Later in the evening, as the shadows creep up the mountain opposite the sinking sun, I think back on events past. I think of the day and the past few weeks; of roots and wings and dreams. It's been a grand adventure, one that I'll remember. It's been my first elk season and my first year in the Rockies. I'm a happy hunter and *will be* even if this day, or this season, ends with only the images and close calls I've had so far. As the day grows ever shorter I pull out my glasses and scan the hills hoping a band of wapiti will show me where to be at sunrise tomorrow.

A chipmunk just a few feet away is busy stocking his winter larder. He eyes me for a few cautions moments before scurrying to the cover of a gnarled sagebrush. It's getting cooler now as the sun begins to dip below the horizon. A slight breeze sinks into the canyon, rustling the golden aspen leaves on its decent. The elk should be moving down as well. I flip up my collar and shoulder my pack ready for the mile hike back to camp when, from somewhere out of the growing shadows below, the eerie primal scream of a testosterone drunk bull echoes through the darkening timber.

In this one visceral sound, inseparable in my mind from the mountains themselves, the whole of the western experience can be summed up. Perhaps this sound, and all that it represents – wildness, solitude, solace – is what I've searched for my whole life. Standing here, with darkness bearing down and a bugle ringing in the distance I feel like I've found my place; like I've finally made it home.

Bare Bones

Sunrise. A red sun emerges, thrusting the odd shard of hazy crimson light through a broken wall of fir. Recent fires and a low ceiling create a smoky ambience perfect for capturing those magical first rays. Hanging low over the horizon, the misty haze intercepts, contorts, refracts, and otherwise transforms the mornings light into every possible combination of colorful light from the warm end of the spectrum; sherry red to daisy yellow. The smell of freedom and opportunity hangs heavy in the air; the crisp and resonating calls of the day's earliest risers greet the new day with a chorus fit for royalty. The birds understand my affinity and aren't shy in praising the beginning of a new day. The pale yellow morning light is drenched with sounds of chickadees and robins, the smell of pine pitch, and that palpable electricity that only the hunter knows. This is my time; a time of infinite possibility when you might as well be watching the sun rise a thousand Septembers ago. Why the vast majority of the human race slumbers through this most glorious time of day will forever remain a mystery to me. It is in this pale yellow infancy of day that I stand; stand and wait, awash in one more glorious morning in the Northern Rockies.

Winnegar Hole wilderness area, an obscure little patch of wild and road less land tucked away in northwest Wyoming, bordered on the north by Yellowstone and on the west, Idaho. What a place to be able to play out a dream. The hunt that I've always wanted, the one that I'd fine tuned around so many campfires and lusted over for as long as I can recall, was at hand. Spot and stalk, stick and string black bear, unguided, public land was the reply given to the query over that campfire so many years ago. That's my dream hunt – no big antlers, no guide crowding me, no gadgets, no rush – just a simple, bare bones, down to earth, do it yourself bear hunt. That's what I want!

The sun grows lighter, slowly expanding my little

world, first to the edge of the meadow, then farther. That time is here, when you strain to see, just a little farther, a little deeper into the gloom. At the far edge of the meadow a single large bolder catches my eye, dark in color, oddly animal like in shape. I strain my eyes, but to no avail. Is it moving, or was that my imagination? This ghostly light and a hunter's apprehension sometimes play nasty tricks. A few moments more and I'm certain, I'm peering at the reason I'm in this place. The bear I've dreamed about since traditional archery took hold of my soul and permeated every fiber of my being. The little blacky (chocolate actually) ambles into view from the far side of the glade. After a few moments of excited disbelief, the pounding heart and sweaty palm begin to subside. She's still a hundred yards out and there's scarcely a blade of grass to hide behind. No chance for a stalk here.

With no immediate action at hand, and time to reflect, I kick back and let my mind drift away, back to an account of Osborne Russell traveling through this very country back in the September of 1839. While trapping up in the Yellowstone country with a companion, Russell was relieved of his stock, most of his gear, and coat after falling into a poor position with a band of Blackfoot. He even managed to catch an arrow in the hip and one in the knee for his troubles.

After the skirmish the trappers hobbled, crawled and slid their way south to near Jackson Lake, then west over the divide while battling weakness, hunger and hypothermia, into what is now the Smith wilderness area. Dropping into the Fall River basin and following down stream, the men managed to make the Henry's fork of the Snake and then the 90 miles to Fort Hall. That was a time when you just did what had to be done, no complaints, no excuses. Call me crazy but I'd go back in a heartbeat if I could.

The wind, that up until now has been steady in my face, causes the grouse feather dangling from my bowstring to do a double take. For a second the breeze falters, swaps 180 degrees, and that's all it takes. The tan muzzle goes up, black nose goes to work, beady eyes stare. How keen that nose, one of the best in the wild world, and a bear's defense numero uno. She hesitates a moment – I wouldn't imagine braintan and woodsmoke are common smells to a modern bear – but soon filters out the human underneath and is gone. Gone like a whisper, out of my world; nothing left but a memory.

It's rifle season. Yes, I could be packing a rug about now, filled my tag and gone home. But, what fun would that be? Besides, I've made that mistake once before; back in the southland with the white tail rut in full swing.

I was overlooking a clearcut where, while bowhunting the day before, I had seen a nice buck a fair piece out of my 20 yard range. Sitting with my flintlock (the most modern implement I can bear for big game) across my lap I waited on my buck. Fifteen minutes later the 9 pt. steped from the tree line some 80 yards away. A cock of the hammer, leveling of the sights, squeeze of the trigger and boom, there lay my buck, still as stone. Man what a hunt! Right. A fine trophy lay at my feet but all I could feel was regret. I had just let the talk of big antlers and such rob me of the opportunity to hunt that animal. I had forgone the match of cunning; the use of all my hard won woodcraft; the excitement of being breath holding close. All for a set of antlers I thought I'd be proud of.

I thought I had wanted the animal more than the hunt. Oh how wrong I was. I felt as though I had gained nothing but a dead deer; meat in the freezer, but not the trophy I was looking for. That deer is the only animal that I've ever killed that I was disappointed in – probably more in myself than the animal. He was a young buck with a lot of potential, a buck that would have been a real trophy with my bow, but I cheated myself into carrying my rifle instead of my beloved longbow. The bow is what I love, and if hunting with it sometimes means unfilled tags, then so be it. I don't ever want to feel that sickening disappointment again.

Back at camp that night, with that particularly lovely light which only firelight through canvas can emit, I lay thinking about the day; about the bear and the buck from years ago; about myself and the men who made this country. An overwhelming feeling of nostalgia took hold. That's one of the great things about hunting for pure love of the hunt. Feelings of connection, solitude, and solace come strong. Earlier in the week, I came across a track, the first of its kind I'd ever seen. Wide as my hand is long, with five toes and a claw an inch in front of each. I knew there were grizzlies in the area but now it felt all so real. I became a little more alert; a little more aware, and consequently a little better at my game. What more could a romantic nut want than to be draped in braintan buckskin, hunting with a handmade yew longbow, camped in the shadow of the Teton with just enough grizzly sign around to keep things a little edgy.

A month ago I began some serious research into bear hunting. Where I come from it's all pine trees, white tails, and wild turkeys so, when I came west, I didn't know squat. After talking to some folks, perusing the fish & game web sites, and reading some old magazine articles one common theme began to emerge: find the berries; ya find the berries, ya find the bears. Easy enough I thought.

I'll just do a little scouting, find a nice patch of serviceberries, and wait – just like hunting white tails at a white oak. Armed with my newly acquired insight into black bear ecology I set off on what was to be the first weekend of my three weekend hunt. The first day I searched high and low for a decent patch of berries. I looked in draws, on ridges, near streams and everywhere else I could imagine but to no avail. After the second fruitless (literally) day of searching I decided a plan B was in order. The only problem was, I didn't really have a plan B.

None of my sources mentioned anything about what to do in a drought year when all you can find is a few shriveled mountain ash berries, and one single bear turd in two days. While driving out Sunday evening, feeling beat and wondering what to do, plan B stood up about 70 yards off the forest service road. The chocolate bear was standing on hind legs, eying the truck as I slowed to a halt and groped for the binoculars in the seat beside me. We looked at one another for a short moment then he dropped down and loped out of sight.

I put the truck in park and walked out into the little meadow where the bear was standing. Knee high sedge grew thickly from the moist soil, there were a few tracks and some torn up soil where the bear had been digging some sort of roots. Huh... roots, never thought of that! When I got back to the truck I opened up my topo maps and picked out every spot I could find like the one I'd just found. I could hardly wait till the next weekend.

Three weeks into the season with a few failed stalks, lots of lessons learned and only one "harvested" sow away from this unit being closed for the season (Wyoming manages its black bear units by female quota. Once a pre determined number of sows are killed, the unit is closed for the season) I found myself with only 50 yards between my buckskin clad self and a chocolate sow and what may have been my last chance to fill my tag. She was in a smallish meadow, just like the one I'd seen that Sunday evening on the first weekend.

Everything was the same except that the wind was in my face and she hadn't a clue I was there. The soft deerskin moccasins made barely a rustle as I slipped through the firs down to the edge of the willow ringed glade. Skirting the edge, moving into position, with just a narrow wall of willows between us, I could see her. Her face was down, covered by the dense sedges. She was making a bit of noise carelessly rustling in the dry vegetation, ignorant of the danger stalking so close. The last rays of sun poured into the meadow highlighting the golden sedge and accentuating her long, milk chocolate fur. Three more cautious steps and I made it to a break in the willows only 5 yards from that beautiful brown black bear; a mere fifteen feet from fulfilling a long time fantasy. I remember those last few moments through a dreamlike veil; the bowstring coming back, the arrow streaking away, disappearing into the dark chest, the dull chuck of the striking shaft. When was the last time a scene like this played out? A buckskin clad hunter just feet from his quarry, bow at full draw, life and death in the balance. The bear giving her life to the skills and hard won knowledge of the hunter, the hunter giving praise to the bear in that eternal struggle for life. Old as time.

The sun is going down, signaling with some mysterious level of ambient light known only to the birds, the start of the evening chorus. The chickadees, always jubilant, sing the days adventures, or perhaps argue the best route to the wintering grounds. It's getting cooler now, and with the last of the meat in the pack, it's time to be headed home.

I started this season with a goal in mind: to fill my bear tag and carry out a dream; to do so without regret, in a way that felt right to me. I came away with a filled tag, full heart, and a grand adventure to sing, someday perhaps, when the light is right.

Driftwood

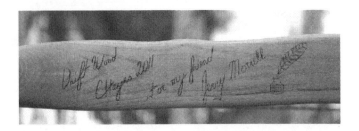

With every pull of the pitted old knife another crenulated curl of paper thin osage, vibrant yellow with youth, drifted to the shop floor. The brick walls of the shop resonated with the hiss of hand forged steel on the dense hardwood stave. A friend tried to give me this stave over a decade ago. And though I couldn't accept it back then, it's somehow found its way here now.

I first met Jerry twelve or maybe thirteen years ago after he'd heard a fellow self bowyer was making shavings in the same county where he lived. We talked on the phone and set a time to meet – I was still in high school, he was recently retired. By that time, I'd made a few bows from locally available materials, persimmon and cedar mostly, but had never even seen a piece of osage, the wood that I'd read about and longed for. Jerry's bow, dark like oiled cherry, was the first osage I'd ever seen. I still remember the iridescence in the wood, almost like you were looking *into* it, below the glassy surface somehow. On that first day, we talked a long while about things we both had known, about bows mostly but other things as well. This man had already done many of the things that I longed to do. He'd been to the Rocky Mountains and far beyond. He was a bowyer, bladesmith, fletcher, and general dinosaur – a relic in affinity and philosophy. I'd never met anyone like him, someone with whom I could identify so readily.

Up until just recently this stave that I'm working on now stood in the dusty corner of Jerry's shop. Tucked in behind bundles of river cane and rolls of rawhide it stood gathering dust and darkness with age, out of sight and out of mind. I'd first lay eyes on it at the Tannahill shoot in central Alabama not long after we'd first met. It was my first 3D shoot and first time being around other traditional shooters other than Jerry. He'd placed the stave in the back of the truck for the drive up from north Florida, saying it was going back to the man he'd got it from.

When we arrived at the shoot, that man was sitting in a lawn chair amid a handful of beautifully wrought self bows and dozens of osage staves. You see Aldridge is a stave dealer, or was back then, and a connoisseur of fine osage. A later visit to his central Alabama home revealed hundreds, if not a thousand or more, neatly cut and stacked osage staves, their ends sealed with clear glue so you could see the growth rings. Each was marked with a date but some had other marks. One indicated that it was a sister stave to another that had made a fine bow, others hinted at secret groves where they'd been cut.

A few more scrapes and the stave is beginning to take on the graceful lines of a bow. It's been pretty easy as far as an osage stave goes. But what else could you expect from such a perfect stave. Years ago, Aldredge had already removed the bark and sapwood down to a single unbroken yearly ring which, like the hundreds of others he'd cut, bore a mark. But this mark was different. It wasn't a date or a place or anything else but something special. Something about this piece had caught his eye and upon the already finished back he scribed just three words, "NOT FOR SALE". I knew what those words meant a decade ago at Tannahill and I know even more intimately now with every scrape. Aldredge had intended to make a bow from this stave – with its perfect lines and backset, it's tight rings and hefty weight – but somehow Jerry had ended up with it and he had intended to return it at Tannahill a decade ago.

By the time we'd all met at Tannahill, Aldredge and Jerry had known each other for many years. Jerry introduced Aldredge and I, and we all shot a round, by the end of which I felt like I'd know them both for years. We sat around and talked, or rather they talked and I listened, about old times; about past hunts and wood and bows.

Jerry left for a few moments leaving me to quiz Aldredge about the various qualities of osage. Upon his return he carried the perfect stave that read not for sale. He then told Aldredge that "about ten years ago, when I was up to get some staves, I picked this one out of your stack. I've felt bad about it ever sense. So here, it's yours." And with that action, Jerry set this particular stave on a swirling tide of giving that took it from Aldredge to me and back to Jerry and a long ride back to the dusty shop corner in north Florida. That was over 12 years ago.

Since that time, I've moved across the country, bought a house, got married, had kids, and made no telling how many bows. Aldredge and Jerry stayed put, their roots firmly planted in southern soil. A few months ago, while back home visiting, I went to Jerry's place to shoot a little and catch up. Before I said goodbye, we went to his shop and sifted through a dozen or so osage staves, most of which he and I had cut several years before. He said he would never get around to using them all and wanted me to have them so we started placing them in the back of the truck.

We eventually came to the one marked "not for sale". The staves perfect lines and backset, so uncharacteristic of osage, made it instantly recognizable even though I'd not seen it in over a decade. Jerry pulled the stave out and asked if I remembered it. "Of course I remember it. Who could forget a stave like that?" We talked a while; about the wood and the day at Tannahill where it changed hands so many times and ended up back where it had begun. I thought this stave much like a piece of driftwood. Felled by a bowers saw and tangled in the brush for years before being set adrift, down the tide, to find its way into the brambles of another bowers dusty shop. There, only to sit for many more years before being cast out into a swirling eddy again, and again. A piece of osage turned dark with age yet still embryonic on its journey to becoming a bow. I told Jerry I'd take the stave if only it could someday find its way back to him.

And so I'm here now, about to package this left handed bow that I'll never be able to shoot properly. The making has been easy; almost effortless as the shavings fell away from the bow that lay inside. I've never worked with a piece of wood that begged to be a bow like this one. And now, 25 years after

Aldredge first cut this perfect stave, it's done. All the hacking, shaving and sanding; the tillering, inscribing, and sealing are finished, and the first arrow launched. It will soon be set adrift again, back to Jerry as the bow that was there all along. But this time, I suspect, it won't be gathering dust behind the rawhide and river cane.

Redemption

It's an affliction; a disability that raises its ugly head at the most inopportune times. It affects your memory – long term, ingrained, and hard won memories. They just disappear when you need them most. Mine had been in remission for over ten years until this last fall when it came back with a vengeance. Buck fever is the most common name among hunters. It's "performance anxiety" to the rest of the world.

I thought I'd had mine under control, and indeed I did, or do, for whitetails. It was a big bull elk that brought on this last bout. He was standing there broadside at 15 yards, an easy as pie shot, but I managed to screw it up. The only thing I remember doing right is hitting full draw. After that, everything went to hell. I didn't pick a spot. I didn't get my eye down over the arrow. I didn't do anything I needed to do to hit where I wanted. The result was a wounded elk, a fruitless search, and a sickening, sleepless night.

I used to have it bad, back when I first started hunting whitetails with a longbow. It took me three years to finally kill a doe, but it wasn't for lack of opportunity. I missed deer after deer, often from nearly point blank range, before finally connecting. I probably missed ten deer in those first 3 years and somehow managed to not wound anything. Clean misses all, and I'm thankful for that. Those misses though, could easily have been gut shot deer.

It wasn't that I was a poor shot. A 3-D course didn't stand a chance and I regularly killed small game at distances greater than what I had missed all those deer at. Big game, even though most were whitetail does, brought on a serious flare-up in buck fever. Finally though, on one cool November evening in Alabama, it all came together. I saw the spot, that one single and all important spot behind her shoulder and never took my eyes off it.

After killing that first doe, something changed. My affliction subsided and I never had another problem. That is, until this last fall. I felt that same disappointment at having botched an easy shot, only this time it was accompanied by the sickening feelings over a wounded animal. Disgusting is the term that comes to mind, though it hardly does justice to the feelings. Thousands upon thousands of arrows, and time equating to years, I've spent in preparation for that one single moment – a chance – like the one I had.

I've used mental imagery, imagined exactly the sequence of events, the actions I'd take, when an animal comes in. I'd thought it through a hundred times but seemingly nothing could prepare me for that moment. Caught in the open, hunkered close to the ground, trying to look like the knee high pines that surrounded us with a bull literally standing over me at five yards. I was a nervous wreck, thinking the bull would catch me at any second and leave me there, hunkered and holding my bow – arrow still nocked. He did catch me, wheeled and ran but stopped at 15 yards, broadside. When he stopped I was already drawn. But instead of picking a spot, instead of doing what needed to be done, my mind raced with thoughts of him bolting again. I watched his eyes for signs of flight and pulled my shot because of it. The arrow struck hard in the base of the neck.

Since then, I've made a change in the way I look at animals. Our first tendency is to see the eyes, and then the rest. It's been a struggle to break this habit, but I've shifted my concentration to the spot, the pocket, in the crease of the shoulder. The eyes are important – the head position, the body language – but they can be accounted for peripherally. The important point, the do or die spot, is behind the shoulder. I've started looking at animals as radiating from there instead of the eye. In this new way I look at my dogs, my horses, and the deer across the field, and it's helped to develop a new habit.

About two months after the elk disaster, I was zoned in on a tuft of hair as big as a watermelon, or so it seemed, tight behind the shoulder of a young doe. The ruffled spot, probably no bigger than a quarter, stood out in crystal clarity and big in my mind's eye. Much bigger and clearer even than I remembered on any of the other animals I'd taken. The arrow passed clean through and I found it sticky and blood soaked, sticking from the ground and marking the spot where she had stood a few moments before.

I thanked, and field dressed the doe, reflecting on the moment of clarity and the feeling that comes with a well placed arrow and a quick, clean kill. I

thought about a wounded bull, a new way of seeing,
and was thankful for the blood on my hands.

Tan yer Hide

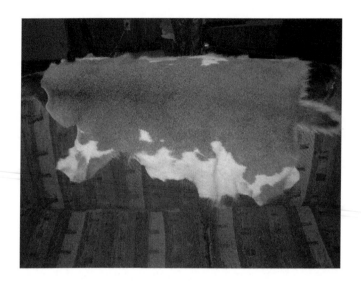

Hide tanning is an art that, along with fire, stone tools, and the like, helped to make us into who we are today. We've developed methods of preserving animal skins ranging from the most primitive, yet sophisticated, brain tanning, to the most modern chemical emersions common to today's leather industry. What follows is an exceedingly simple, easy, and cheap way to turn your next deer hide into a supple and attractive trophy.

You'll first need to gather a few things. The first

ingredient is, of course, the hide itself. Every year tens of thousands of whitetail hides are discarded. And it just so happens that the hide of a doe or young buck whitetail is one of the easiest hides to tan. It's not too big to be cumbersome. It's thick enough to resist tearing, but thin enough to easily soften, and it fleshes easily. It seems intuitive that smaller hides, such as squirrels or coons, would be easier but it's just not the case. Smaller critters are easy to preserve, but they're nearly impossible to get soft without using harsh chemical emersions to break down the fibers in the hide. As you'll see, we're going to avoid breaking down the fibers which will result in a much longer lasting and durable end product.

When you pick out a hide, make sure it's not scored. Scoring is when a hide is cut with a knife from the flesh side but not all the way through. These areas are more likely to tear in the softening process later on. I've found that, after you make the initial cuts on a deer – up the legs, the belly, and around the neck, etc. – you can put the knife away and literally pull the hide off. Use your skinning knife sparingly and you'll avoid scoring your hide.

Once you've got a nice hide, you'll need some sort of fleshing tool. With a deer hide, you aren't actually cutting the flesh from the hide, but rather pushing it off. The right angle on the edge of an old lawn mower blade works well after you pad the ends to form handles. Next comes the fleshing beam. A few 2x6s nailed into an A frame configuration works well. The idea is to be able to drape the hide over one of the legs of the A and lean against it with your beltline to hold the hide in place while you push down and away with the fleshing tool. It helps if you round the edges of the board a little to reduce the chances of cutting the hide between the fleshing tool and an abrupt edge on the beam.

Once you've rounded up these things, you'll need a plastic drum, or garbage can, two pounds of salt, and two pounds of alum. You can get alum in bulk at pool chemical supply stores. Also, they sell it along with food preserving items at some grocery stores.

Now that we've gathered all the necessary materials, we can get started. To flesh the hide, lay your A frame fleshing beam on its side so that one of the legs is sticking up. Now you can stand on the lower leg and the upper should reach your beltline. Now drape your hide over the upper, flesh side out and work the meat and fat off from the center out. It should come off pretty easy until you get out to the legs. Here there's only membrane, and it's a real bugger to remove. I don't usually worry about a little membrane left as this will work off during the softening process. Be careful not to score the hide at this stage. You shouldn't need too much pressure to push the flesh off. After the hide is fleshed, it helps to wash it with some laundry detergent and a few changes of water. You'd be amazed at how dirty the water will be.

To mix the tanning solution, simply put about five gallons of warm water in your drum then throw in the salt and alum. Warm water dissolves the salt and alum easier and quicker than cold. Once the solids are mostly dissolved and the solution is cool, put the hide in, give it a few stirs, cover and let simmer for a few weeks. Once the hide's in this solution, it can stay there indefinitely. You're basically pickling it.

While it's soaking you need to stir it every few days initially so the solution can penetrate all portions of the hide. The amount of time needed to fully pickle the hide depends on the temperature. During warm weather, 2 weeks should be more than enough. If it's cold out, two months may not get it done. You can check whether or not the solution has penetrated fully by taking a slice off the edge of a thick part of the hide. Up around the neck is a good place. The color should be uniform all the way through. If your slice reveals a band of color, let it soak longer.

So now you have a preserved hide. We're done right. Now all you have to do is pull it out, dry it and viola, you've got a nice supple hide to drape over the couch. Well, not really. If we did that, the hide would dry into something about as soft as a sheet of plywood. In order to get it soft, we need to a little more work. Actually, that's a little misleading. Now, is when the work really begins.

Before going any farther, I like to rinse the hide again in a few changes of fresh water to get the salt and alum out of the hair. Once this is done, roll the hide up and ring as much water out as you can. It helps to roll and ring it several different ways, top to bottom, left to right, etc. Now, lay it out, flesh side up and apply a light coat of oil. Vegetable oil works well, but neatsfoot oil is made specifically for tanning and leather applications.

Now you'll need a few hours you can devote to pulling and stretching the hide until it's completely dry and soft. By pulling and stretching the hide while it's drying, you're not allowing the fibers in the hide to stick together. Moving into the sunshine seems like a good way to speed the drying process, but it's also a good way to a stiff hide. Sorry, but there's no shortcuts in this process. The thinner portions of the hide will dry sooner, and as they do, they'll turn darker. Stretching these areas will lighten them like magic.

Sometimes it helps to break the hide over the corner

of a table to stretch difficult areas. If you can't stretch the hide until absolutely bone dry, stick it in a plastic bag in the fridge or freezer until you can finish. When the hide is nearly completely dry, it often helps to cable it. Cabling is a final step involving rapidly pulling a hide back and forth over a tight cable or rope. This really helps to loosen those hide fibers and give a super soft hide.

Home Butchering

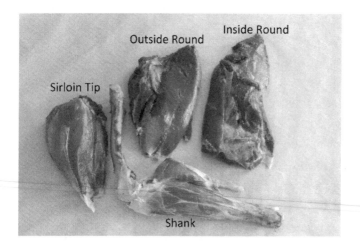

Butchering our own game is an easy and satisfying opportunity to further our involvement in taking an animal from the field to the freezer. Besides being easier on the checkbook, home butchering lets us decide exactly what cuts and portions suit our individual needs while getting all the same cuts you'd get from a professional. Here's how.

Ageing

Ageing meat is an important, yet often neglected, step in producing tender, flavorful cuts. The ageing process allows natural enzymes to breakdown the

71

hard connective tissue in meats and for water to evaporate away concentrating the flavor. Most meat packing houses that age beef, hang halves in walk in coolers at somewhere between 32 and 36 degrees.

If you've got a meat locker, that's great but the backyard butcher rarely has such luxuries – so we make due. When the weather is cool, but not too far below freezing, (between 28 and about 38 deg is good) I like to hang quarters where they will be well protected; out of the wind and sun, and away from prowling critters but in a well ventilated area. I'll hang quarters from 2 days to a week or more, depending on conditions. To get it right takes a bit of practice so it may be advisable to start small until you've got a feel for the process. A little darkening around the edges of the meat is normal but if the meat begins to smell funky, you've gone too far.

If you're down south, it's early season, or you're otherwise experiencing conditions that won't allow for outdoor hanging, you can accomplish the same thing by aging individual cuts in the fridge for a few days before cooking. Ageing all sorts of game, from ducks to moose, is important if you want to get the most from your cuts.

Cutting

After a few days on the meat pole, and assuming the critter is in quarters, we'll separate the muscle groups of the hams into the various cuts. Starting with the ham on a table, inside up, find the femur (big bone, top of leg or thigh) and make a cut along the natural seam from the knee joint to the ball of the hip. This will expose the entire femur. Continue to trim around this bone, taking care to keep your cuts close to the bone itself, until it is free and connected only at the knee.

Now make a cut perpendicular to the femur, just above the knee, to separate this large, boneless chunk (which is made up of the sirloin tip, inside & outside rounds) from the shank. At this point, separating the large muscle groups will yield the sirloin tip, inside round, and outside round. I like to cut the rounds into thick steaks and leave the sirloin tip for a roast. As for the shank and all the leftover trimmings from the steaks and roasts, cut it into cubes for stew or grind into burger later on.

One important thing to watch for when throwing trimmings in the grind bowl is glands. There is a big one just behind the knee right at the top of the shank. It's incased in a mass of fat and membrane. You don't want this ending up in your burger. On deer sized game I just cut the meat off the shoulders and either grind it or cut it in chunks for stew, etc. For me, there's just not enough meat to make a good roast or steaks.

The tender loins (not to be confused with back straps) are the equivalent of filet mignon. They're located in the inside of the body cavity above the kidneys and along the spine. On a 150 pound whitetail, they'll be a little smaller than the diameter of a tennis ball and about a foot long. Just keep them whole and wrap them up. They're great on the grill, and fork tender. The backstrap takes a little more prep work before going into the freezer.

We'll need to remove the sinew (dry and save for all sorts of uses later on) before cutting. Start by laying the strap on a large cutting board or table with the sinew side down and the butt end of the strap toward you. Now just filet the meat from the sinew like you would take the skin off a big fish. A good, sharp filet knife really helps here. Once the sinew is removed, I like to cut steaks around an inch and a half thick or so. I cut them thick to allow for pounding or punching them out before cooking. You can punch out a thick 4 inch steak to about 6 inches diameter.

Now that we're done with all the major parts, we'll talk about everything else. A neck roast from a whitetail buck is one of the best roasts on the whole critter. I just cut a cross section of the neck down near the base to include 3 or 4 vertebra. This will give you a roast about 6 inches thick or so that's mighty fine in the crock pot with some carrots, taters and onions. I've fairly limited experience with elk but, from the ones I've butchered, the neck meat isn't much for roasts. It tends to have a lot of chewy tendon and membrane, but it makes good burger, along with any other meat you can cut off the carcass.

Wrapping

There are lots of ways to wrap meat for freezer storage, from vacuum packaging to plain old butcher paper. Some folks wrap their meat in plastic wrap then butcher paper, but that just seems like a lot of extra work. For me, plain waxed butcher paper works just fine. The key is to cut your paper large enough so that the meat is covered twice as you roll and wrap it up. Also, wrapping tightly helps to keep out freezer burn. Wrapping with butcher paper is quicker, cheaper, works just as well, and stacks better in the freezer than any other method I've tried. And, as long as the meat is tightly wrapped with two layers of paper, freezer burn isn't a problem.

Novels in Nature

*"Every farm is a textbook on animal ecology;
woodsmanship is the translation of the book"
- Aldo Leopold, Sand County Almanac*

Leopold had a wonderful knack for looking at
common things in not so common ways. He saw the
world through a woodsman's eyes and was able to
decipher the relationships between wildlife and
land. The type of farm to which he refers in the
quote above is one of brush piles and hedge rows,
weedy fields and wetlands; one where wildlife
abounds. I've always loved that quote and have

spent the better chunk of my life putting it to action; gaining the skills, acquiring the knowledge, and developing the attitude required to read the kind of stories that Leopold so adeptly translated. Through the woodsman's eye, there are stories in all things – the landscape is full of them. There is a story in every deer track, every bent leaf or turned stone, every tree, every grain of sand; stories written not in words and phrases, but in sign. Once upon a time every hunter had accumulated a fair stash of woodsmanship but sadly, much of that has gone by the wayside.

Woodsmanship isn't some mysterious and unattainable level of skill or knowledge. It isn't a lost art only to be read about in history books. What it *is*, is a continuum; a sliding scale of knowledge – attained and solidified, and skills – tested and honed. Having the skills – camping, orienteering, reading sign, etc. – isn't woodsmanship in itself, but woodcraft. Woodsmanship is knowing when, where and how to employ those skills, and the woodsman is the seasoned practitioner. I don't know at what level you begin to call a hunter or fisherman or outdoors person a woodsman, but I'd argue that he or she must have acquired at least a basic level of woodcraft and, most importantly, a passion for things wild and natural. It's that passion, after all, which drives us to continue learning and practicing.

So what makes a woodsman? Is it knowledge? How about skill in a particular area? I'd say no on both counts because woodsmanship cannot be bought in a book or taught in a classroom. Woodcraft can be taught, and values instilled, but woodsmanship can only be had through experience. Woodsmanship, and the title that goes with it, must be earned. It must be paid for in blood and sweat, hot and cold, days in the field and nights in camp. No book or classroom can replace that.

You don't have to be a hunter to be a woodsman, though most woodsmen are. You simply need to be an astute observer and a willing student of Mother Nature's lessons. She is willing to teach, but you have to be out there to learn. Above all, the woodsman is a naturalist and a student. Woodsmanship has no upper bounds and if a woodsman were to live with nature a hundred years he could learn something about her on his last day, just as his first. Nature is a complex lady and there are no limits to her depth, but only limits to our ability to comprehend.

Sadly, woodsmen are an endangered lot. Once upon a time, to be a hunter was to be a woodsman. Not long ago – when little boys played cowboys and Indians in the woodlot out back, and idolized Disney's version of Davy Crockett – woodsmanship was still part of every family camping trip and day in the woods. Woodcraft was taught at an early age, campers slept in tents or under the stars, hunters became familiar with their quarry, woodsmanship was alive. Not so for most in this day in age, and that's a tragic loss.

So what happened? Where *have* all the woodsmen gone? Today, Spongebob and the Power Rangers have taken the place of Davy Crockett. There's now a subdivision where the woodlot once stood. "Campers" stay in luxury homes on wheels, complete with big screen TV, X-Box 360, and satellite dish. Some "hunters" drive their ATVs around and hope to see a critter to shoot with the latest high-tech weaponry while others pay guides to be the woodsmen. It's more convenient that way, which brings up a good point. It seems like most hunters today are more concerned with convenience and comfort than with hunting. Since when did convenience and comfort creep into a hunter's vocabulary anyway?

But I digress. Modern humanity's perceived need for these things isn't the intent of this essay. I don't want to linger on the past and present, but to give hope for the future.

As bleak as the state of many modern hunters sometimes seems, woodsmanship, though probably not at the level it once was, is alive in the hearts of most hunters. Most, no matter what they carry in their hand, have at least a little woodcraft tucked away in their rusty old brains. And, with more and more hunters becoming fed up with technology, there seems to be a slight trend toward more traditional and skillful ways of hunting. A lot of us have come to realize that when we set aside those crutches we've been coerced into believing we need, and challenge ourselves, some of that corrosion begins to flake off, the gears begin to turn, and apathy dissolved. Latent, and perhaps innate, skills are developed and sharpened. Nature is a great solvent for all the gunk that clogs a hunters head. We just need to rid ourselves of all the crap that insulates us from her.

I mentioned before that woodsmanship is a continuum; it is acquired and built upon, sometimes in small subtle bits of insight and sometimes in a sudden moment of enlightenment. About 15 years ago I began making and hunting with wood bows and so began some of the best training I could ever imagine. There's something about traditional archery that nurtures woodsmanship. Maybe it's the slower pace and simplicity that such a weapon demands that direct our attention to the seemingly little things in nature and ourselves. Perhaps the type of people traditional bowhunting attracts are just more inclined to take notice. That could be part of it, but I have another theory.

I think it's the simple fact that we're often able to spend the entire season chasing game around the forest with little risk of having to pack meat (well, me anyhow). Long after the compound guys have come and gone, lugging those cumbersome antlers down the trail (oh how I pity them), we're out there; sneaking, watching, trying like hell to close the distance. Had I hunted with a compound this past elk season, I probably could have killed that raghorn that came into the wallow on opening weekend, or one of the three cows that walked past me the second, or any of the several other animals I got to within 50 yards of.

But then I wouldn't have been out there on the last weekend. I wouldn't have felt the excitement of calling in a 45-inch Shiras bull moose to 10 yards. I wouldn't have been there to sit out a thunder storm on the lee side of a windswept ridge, trying like hell to keep my rawhide-backed bow dry. I would never have played a half-hour game of cat and mouse with two mulie does in the snowbrush, thinking they were elk, and I couldn't have added those little diamonds of insight to my woodsmanship stash. It's often the little things, the seemingly unimportant tidbits that make all the difference.

On another, more recent, adventure I had one of

those big "Ah ha!" moments that we all get from time to time. I was on a spot and stalk hunt for black bears and was having a difficult time spotting anything to stalk. All the research I'd done on fall bears said to concentrate on berry patches. I tried that for the first two days and wasn't able to find much in the way of berries or bears. In all of my reading and research, I hadn't come across anything that said what to do in a drought year when the berry crop was in the toilet.

Figuring out what to do would take an adaptive approach and time in the woods. While driving out Sunday evening, I found the answer and gained a little ground on the woodsmanship scale. I was headed home when a bear stood up in a meadow just off the shoulder of the Forest Service road. After the little blackie headed for safer ground I walked out to where she had been and discovered she'd been digging roots in the moist soil. I pulled out my stack of topo maps and marked every little meadow like the one where the bear had been.

I changed my strategy and started stalking these little meadows from downwind and checking them for bears. Over the next eight days I saw eight more bears and seven of them were in meadows like the one the little blackie had shown me on that fortuitous Sunday evening. If I hadn't been flexible and learned the lessons that nature offered, I would probably have finished the season with an unfilled tag. But I *was* flexible. I learned and adapted and eventually found myself at full draw, five yards from my bear.

Even though woodsmanship has waned in recent decades, and is being constantly undermined by a gizmo marketing outdoor industry, it's far from dead. Thanks to those blessed souls who honor the old ways, woodsmanship will remain a part of who we are as hunters, and especially traditionalists, even in the face of such things. We will continue to learn and practice, teach and sharpen. And hopefully, when we gain a little on that sliding scale, we'll see fit to pass along a few of those tidbits of knowledge to help the next generations decipher those novels in nature.

Author Bio

Clay Hayes is a professional wildlife biologist, primitive bowhunter, wildlife film maker, and writer. Growing up on his family's farm in the Florida panhandle, he spent his boyhood summers among the cypress swamps and Spanish moss. But, as alluring as southern woodlands are, the Rocky Mountains always called. After graduating from Mississippi State University with a masters in wildlife ecology he headed west with his wife to settle among the aspen and endless conifers stretching across the west slope of the continental divide in central Idaho. A lifelong learner, he has always been fascinated with wildlife and has spent the better part of his life studying the ecology of the natural world around him. This fascination, in combination with a love of hunting, eventually led him to the world of traditional and primitive archery. Limiting the effectiveness of his weapons allows him to gain an intimate knowledge of the game he pursues, and the myriad other creatures encountered along the way. Clay lives in central Idaho with his wife Liz and two boys, Coye and Fen.

In 2012, in an attempt to preserve and promote woodsmanship and traditional skills, Clay started twistedstave.com. On his website, you'll find the best video instructions on building archery equipment anywhere, and it's absolutely free. There is also a link to his youtube channel where you'll find more how-to outdoor videos.

A note from Clay

Thank you for purchasing this book. If you've got suggestions for future books, or videos, I'd love to hear from you. You can contact me at clay@twistedstave.com

If you enjoyed this book, and purchased it on Amazon, please leave a 5 Star review on there. Good reviews will really help push it to the top where others can find it. You can leave your review by going to your Amazon account and clicking on this book.

Thank you,

ch

Photo Credits

Feral hog – Janet Beasley = JLB Creatives

Prickly pears –ikewinski. This photo was cropped and color corrected.

Treestand – dooneling

All others – Clay & Elizabeth Hayes

Creative Commons (CC) license can be found at:
http://creativecommons.org/licenses/by/2.0/legalcode